PRAISE FOR
Transforming Everyday Conflict

Alberta Fredricksen provides the perfect tools to create stronger and more fulfilling relationships in all areas of our life. Her wise and practical tips should be a part of everyone's survival kit.

—Patricia Spadaro, author of *Honor Yourself: The Inner Art of Giving and Receiving*

This is the most complete and comprehensive book on conflict resolution I've ever read. Alberta has it down. Her fresh and positive view on conflict as natural and normal instead of bad and barely endurable provides the foundation for the many tools, tactics, and training she provides for us to learn how to manage change and conflict. *Transforming Everyday Conflict* is a must-read for all.

—Michael Angier, founder of SuccessNet.org, author of *The Achievement Code*

As an attorney, I search for cogent, succinct, reliable, and credible resources which actually provide useful, practical guidance in resolving conflicts to use and share with clients. A critical question in each conflict is whether the parties are going to craft their own resolution or allow a "disinterested" third party to impose one. Alberta Fredricksen's *Transforming Everyday Conflict* educates and empowers representatives and clients to control and manage the processing of conflicts they will inevitably face. She provides a reliable, real-world framework by which to reach better resolutions. This is one tool which you will definitely keep close at hand.

—Robert Brown, attorney representing employment/labor/healthcare clients

This book is a masterful exposition of the key ingredients for meeting and managing conflict. Practicing them will certainly lead to rich and rewarding relationships and life. If enough people choose so civil a way of meeting disagreement, tension, and conflict as Alberta describes, then truly the world would be one in which cooperation rules and the new age of Aquarian community thrives.

—C.C. Hanstke, psychologist, co-author of *Why We Do What We Do: Understanding Self-Motivation and Psychology of Success*

Transforming Everyday Conflict is a great book that can truly assist all those who work with others. Its wisdom goes beyond the normal psychological approaches of the day and should be required reading in school or college curricula. Instead of running away from conflict or choosing violence to get what we want, this book illustrates a higher way so that all are free to communicate safely and all can find personal worth. This is a foundation of a free society and these tools can be applied in all aspects of life. This masterpiece from the master counselor, mediator, and teacher is easy to understand and provides many techniques and approaches to working through conflicts. I highly recommend this book to anyone truly interested in freeing themselves and all those they assist in taking a higher road to freedom in their lives.

—Rev. Carl Showalter, pastor, counselor, and teacher of spiritual dynamics

The journey of life is fraught with the seeming stumbling stones of conflict. Most of us need a guide to circumnavigate the boulders, and *Transforming Everyday Conflict* is that guide. Alberta Fredricksen is like a skillful shepherd who not only knows the way around these boulders but also straight through them. Her tools and strategies turn what appear to be stumbling stones into stepping stones to learning. Follow her lead, add your own creativity as she advises, and you will be forging greater peace and understanding in relationships all around you.

—Brian Emanuel Grey, co-author of *Why We Do What We Do: Understanding Self-Motivation and Psychology of Success*

Conflict used to scare me. I would bend myself into a pretzel to avoid it, which resulted in resentment and unhappy relationships. Reading *Transforming Everyday Conflict* gave me new tools and confidence to face even the most challenging conflicts and resolve them so that both sides feel great about the solution. Do you need to overcome a fear of conflict? Read this book and you will!

>—Lynne Klippel, bestselling author of *Overcomers, Inc.: True Stories of Hope, Courage, and Inspiration*

Transforming Everyday Conflict is no doubt one of the most comprehensive books written on how to handle oneself in just about every situation where conflict has arisen or could arise. Best of all, it covers the skills one needs in all areas of communication to avoid conflict in the first place. This book could easily be a textbook for study. Bravo to Alberta Fredricksen for so eloquently leading us to the conclusion that conflict is an opportunity for constructive change.

>—Nancy Showalter, Law of Attraction life coach, author, and speaker

Transforming Everyday Conflict correctly identifies change as a constant factor in our lives. Understanding the alchemy of transforming that change in positive ways helps to produce vital and balanced good health. Alberta's book inspires and empowers us to seek understanding in a new way, helping us live from our true, authentic self and offering the same opportunity to others. This is a big step forward in reaping maximum health benefits in all cycles of our life.

>—Marcia Marie Scully, holistic health practitioner

Conflict is everywhere, and no matter how much we want to avoid it, it still happens. That's why Alberta's book is my new go-to resource for better communicating with family, friends, clients, and colleagues. Her book has clear purpose—to help people improve communication, easily resolve conflict with others, and enhance relationships. I especially like the format and easy accessibility of the content with Alberta's "A Choice Tip!", roadmap-type guidelines, and reflections. The quality of her key principles, tips, strategies, and roadmaps is priceless. I highly recommend this book for anyone dealing with conflict situations who would like to improve communication and collaboration with others.

—Kim Clausen, founder of Ready2GoMarketingSolutions, Inc.

Transforming Everyday Conflict

Tools, Tips and Roadmaps to Better Communication and Stronger Relationships

Alberta Fredricksen

HeartPeace Now Publications
Bozeman, Montana

Transforming Everyday Conflict

Copyright © 2014
by Alberta Fredricksen

All rights reserved.

Reproduction or translation of any part of this work beyond that permitted by the 1976 United States Copyright Act without the express written permission of the copyright owner is unlawful. Requests for permission or further information should be addressed to the author at: Alberta@HeartPeaceNow.com

Published by HeartPeace Now
P.O. Box 10312 Bozeman, MT 59719

Library of Congress Control Number: 2014940258
ISBN: 978-1-934509-75-3
Printed in the United States of America

Cover Design by Sarah Barrie of Cyanotype.ca
Editing by Gwen Hoffnagle

For foreign and translation rights, contact Nigel J. Yorwerth
E-mail: nigel@PublishingCoaches.com

This publication is designed to provide accurate and authoritative information in regard to the subject matter covered. It is sold with the understanding that the author is not engaged in rendering professional services. If legal, accounting, medical, psychological, or any other expert assistance is required, the services of a competent professional person should be sought.

Dedication

To all the peacemakers, problem solvers, teachers, and community builders in my life for keeping the faith, holding higher intentions and a steady balance, and gently leading through wisdom and right confrontation to create greater understanding, stronger relationships, more and better communication, and a shared responsibility for community—I am grateful!

Table of contents

Acknowledgments 13
Introduction 15
How to Use This Book 23

CHAPTER 1: *Three Powerful Keys to Understanding Conflict* 31
CHAPTER 2: *The Power of Choice* 39
CHAPTER 3: *Seeking and Offering Forgiveness* 43
CHAPTER 4: *Seven Tips for Managing Your Own History during Conflict* 53
CHAPTER 5: *Five Mistakes to Avoid during Conflict* 57
CHAPTER 6: *The Art and Science of Giving Directions* 61
CHAPTER 7: *Basic Steps for Problem-Solving* 71
CHAPTER 8: *How to Make Tough Decisions* 75
CHAPTER 9: *How to Deal with Another's Anger* 79
CHAPTER 10: *The Art of Listening* 89
CHAPTER 11: *How to Give Information* 97
CHAPTER 12: *Handling Complaints* 101
CHAPTER 13: *Fist to Five Process for Consensus-Building* 105
CHAPTER 14: *Some Closing Thoughts: Think Courage!* 113

APPENDIX A: *A Simple Action Plan* 123
APPENDIX B: *When and How to Use a Summary Memorandum* .. 127
About the Author 131

Acknowledgments

Writing and publishing a book on managing and resolving conflict is the work of a great many people. While holding a book like this in your hands, you see only one author's name on the cover. However, the contents are truly like a patchwork quilt made by a worldwide community. The principles, tips, tools, and strategies represent precious scraps of fabric from the lives of many people and the life experiences we have forged and shared together in our common experience, and they come together as a whole cloth.

While thanking and acknowledging everyone who has contributed to this effort is impossible, I begin with my parents. We were a *regular* family and both my parents worked outside the home. I know there must have been conflicts and disagreements, and yet as a child I never witnessed my parents fighting. I learned that things were serious and I had made a big mistake when *both* my parents sat me down to talk about some incident or aspect of my behavior. I believe that this set a pattern for my life that most things could be resolved and worked through with good communication and strong relationships.

From my decades of experience as a teacher, school site administrator, organizational and union leader, and human resources administrator, I want to gratefully acknowledge all the individuals who filed grievances and sat at bargaining tables to hammer out agreements in labor negotiations; all the students, parents, and staff who presented problems requiring some level of resolution; and the skillful attorneys who advised me and those who advised my adversaries. And as a conflict coach and minister, I thank all those who were courageous enough to confront issues—complex, difficult, transitioning, and resolving—both within themselves and with others, and who remained willing to seek reconciliation, cooperation, and a sense of community. They have all been my teachers.

I offer my deepest and enduring gratitude to all the friends and spiritual family who have supported me and all my efforts through many years.

For the physical completion of this book, I am grateful to Lynne Klippel as a teacher, writing coach, editor, designer, and publisher.

Introduction

We live in a conscious universe where everything is connected and every situation is driven by potential.

—Dr. Vernon Woolf, Founder and Director of the International Academy of Holodynamics

Conflict is a gift that just keeps on giving! "You've got to be kidding, right?" That's what some of my clients say when I introduce this concept to them.

Most of us grow up conditioned to believe that conflict is *bad*. That is a myth! And it's a pretty destructive myth, because it places all of us in a position of being bad in some way when we experience conflict, either within ourselves or with others.

I really never met anyone who was trained in managing conflict while they were growing up. It isn't offered in elementary schools—and it should be.

Conflict is natural and normal, and it's all around us. Have you ever wondered how those magnificent mountain ranges with their jagged peaks, steep walls, waterfalls, and deep lakes were formed? They were formed by earth upheavals, wind, and rain coming together in conflict—and sometimes violent encounters that changed things forever, with beautiful and undreamed-of results! Thomas Crum, Aikido Master and author of *The Magic of Conflict: Turning a Life of Work into a Work of Art*, says that *conflict is nature's primary motive for change.*

Managing conflict is managing change!

We have all faced the world, and out of necessity we developed our own coping mechanisms that somehow just don't cope. We learned from one another but we did not have the benefit of a core curriculum in embracing change and conflict as something to learn and master as we did with reading and math. How different our world might be if we had received instruction and a chance to practice and gain a level of mastery in managing change and conflict and harmonizing relationships—all the while fully realizing our connectedness with one another.

Most of us can identify with having feelings and thoughts about how things or people need to change to better fit our model of how our world should be. We tell others how we wish things were. We want change. We might even pray for change in our lives and in the lives of those around us. We are actually longing for some kind of transformation or transmutation to make things different than they are. One of my teachers used to say, "Transformation is just a fancy word for change." We are *calling* for change!

Then why are we so surprised when things change? Why are we so surprised when people change? And why do we resist change—kicking at the pricks when our level of status quo is upset? As human beings we get comfortable with our patterns, habits, momentums, and even the addictions that don't serve us well. And even though we want circumstances or people to change, if they do it without us or in a way that we did not prescribe, it's upsetting—even threatening. And we experience conflict.

It's not too late. We can still change the world and our own lives by learning to appreciate the benefits and gifts that can come from carefully managed opportunities for change. Opportunities for change definitely include the conflict we find inhabiting our lives. And, yes! Conflict *is* an opportunity for change—and that makes it a gift!

> **Note from "William":** *What a different world this would be if this training were in schools. I hope that you and your "people" can help this happen. If I had*

had this back then, I would not have given or received so much heartache.

A change is needed

I like to think of conflict as a messenger who knocks on your door. The messenger is sent to get your attention. *A change is needed.*

A conflict shows up and demands your focus and energy. This presents you with an important choice. Will you see the conflict as an unfair, interruptive event that you must immediately blame on something or someone other than you in order to feel right or be okay? Or will you see it as new information—an opportunity for a course correction that can transform you and your world?

If you want to accomplish your mission in this life, it is not so much about where you are going but about the changes you will go through to get there.

An ancient leader named Pericles once said, "What you leave behind is not what is engraved in stone monuments, but what is woven into the lives of others."

> **Note from "Maria":** *Conflict is worse than a dental visit or the flu because the "sufferer" knows there's an end to the discomfort of the flu or dental visit. However, conflict can last a lifetime or bring an end to the life of relationships. It steals peace of mind and energy. And underneath it, even if we think or believe that we are right, it shakes our self-esteem. When our concept of self doesn't include a wider and longer vision of who we are and who the "adversary" is, life can feel like a sentence instead of an adventure.*

"Maria" artfully expressed her maturing view of conflict. This is a demonstration of expanded awareness that comes from looking more deeply at the opportunities and gifts that conflict brings. In her note to me she also wrote that even though she might not remember all the conflict resolution concepts in the midst of the fray of conflict, she now knows there is a way to understand. She can go back and review the principles and the steps. And she feels empowered when she can expand her concern and goodwill to both sides.

She said, "We're in this for a higher reconfiguration. I am able to adjust my point of view, my understanding and tolerance of the differences...it helps me believe the best in me and in others and then the techniques and information can sink in better because I can dare to care and still be safe and not mind changing myself, which is the moving of mountains."

Can you remember having an exchange with someone that you felt did not go so well? Perhaps later you found yourself going over and over it in your mind, thinking of things you could have said or wish you had said. But in that moment of tension or discomfort—perhaps even sensing being in danger or being made to feel wrong— you just couldn't think of that good response. And you did not know what to do at that moment. What you do know is that it didn't feel good. Something in the relationship was interrupted, damaged, or broken. And now you don't know where you stand in the relationship. Your peace has been stolen and your energy has been sidetracked.

Just *being* in conflict is truly as easy as falling off a log! And any one of us can choose to do it all day long with disastrous results for our attitude, our sense of self, our connectedness to others, and our productiveness. With a little shift in perception, an understanding of the true nature of conflict, and some communication skill sets, you can choose to walk the log skillfully and reap the benefits of harmonized relationships. Then you can experience the opportunities that conflict provides for managing changes and making things new!

I remember my grandmother saying to me when I was eleven or twelve, "Honey, you should become a lawyer when you grow up." I asked, "Why?" She said, "Because you always have the right words to say." All of us have many conversations each day—sometimes hundreds of them. We all have a desire to *connect* with one another. That's what communication really is. When we truly connect with another person and they really get what we are trying to share with them, we *feel* good. And *they* feel good. We experience a sense of understanding, rapport, and kinship with that other person. Our communications build relationships that can transcend isolation and highlight our connectedness.

While I did not pursue that legal career my grandmother suggested when I was a child, my path has brought me into contact with many varieties of tension and conflict. And it is through these encounters that I have come to have more than just a grudging respect for conflict as a gift—a gift of true opportunity—opportunity for managing change, choosing to create something new, and healing and strengthening relationships.

In my decades of working with diverse individuals and groups in public education, labor negotiations, mediation,

Alberta Fredricksen

a prison system, coaching, and ministry, I have been privileged to know many individuals, including some fine attorneys and other personal advocates, who did know the right things to say in circumstances in which conflict was present. They understood that choosing to improve communication strategies can help resolve or more effectively manage conflict. They have all been my teachers!

I still have enduring relationships that were formed during times of conflict or crisis. And the longevity of these relationships has to do with the levels of integrity we won together, under duress. We experienced a greater sense of self and appreciation of others through learning how to communicate, listen, be heard, and share in creating new outcomes, while honoring everyone's offering. They, too, have been my teachers, and I am grateful!

How to use this book

*Communication leads to community; that is,
to understanding, intimacy and mutual valuing.*

—Rollo May, American psychologist

During episodes of conflict we are led to learning new ways of talking, listening, providing feedback, and relating to others—those with whom we agree or disagree. We learn—often the hard way—that relationships count! We have opportunities in our lives, families, businesses, communities, and nations to grow our relationships—our interconnectedness—even with people half a world away or with the Earth itself. We can learn to problem-solve together, resolve differences, and create new ways of being with one another. What it takes is an expanded consciousness and more and better communication!

We must progress past old patterns of communicating, old feelings, and former ways of thinking that we still engage in simply because they are habitual. The old momentums are heavy—almost like gravity, holding us down and anchored. In short, we need to cut loose and create some new habits!

Although there are many books and courses available on conflict resolution or conflict management, the purpose of this book is to offer some key principles, tips, strategies, and roadmaps that actually work to improve communication without doing harm to relationships. Some are in the form of checklists that are simply roadmaps to give you general direction. Some offer formulas for the important steps needed to navigate specific types of conflict. None of them are mandates.

Some ideas and quotes are labeled **A Choice Tip!** Always remember that **A Choice Tip!** means you get to choose and you are in charge at that moment. The power of choice is so important in transforming conflict. Your own creativity and inner guidance is essential! And it's a great idea to invite and capitalize on the creativity and inner guidance of others who might be sharing with you this experience of shifting conflict to an opportunity to create something new.

The tips, tools, and strategies described in this book are meant to provide some structure for identified types of conflict; however, *you* are the *essential* ingredient as you *stay present*, focus, analyze and assess, adapt, and then effectively manage or overcome a conflict by arriving at a new outcome.

It might be helpful to consider the unofficial mantra of the U.S. Marines Corps: Improvise, Adapt, and Overcome. In their earliest beginnings the Marines were equipped with hand-me-downs from the Army that were often substandard. So they were taught a *culture of success*. They were expected to *improvise, adapt,* and *overcome.*

The roadmap-type guidelines are intended to get your creative juices flowing. Remember that a conscious, present person is the solution to each problem. Just think of what you can do with a room full of conscious, present people aligned for a common purpose, cause, or goal!

We are in a new age—a time of boundless technology and millions of creators and entrepreneurs endlessly creating worldwide. All of this requires some degree of cooperation, coordination, and *harmonization of relationships* through mutual respect as reflected in being present and involved, listening, clarifying, and truly understanding others' points of view. They don't call it the *Aquarian* Age for nothing! These attributes provide the necessary elements for managing change and creating new outcomes peacefully, harmoniously, and in ways that have potential for benefitting all involved.

The communication strategies you consciously choose to use create the fabric of your life. They might possess the qualities of cotton, wool, or silk, and by weaving them into your relationships they become the yarn for fashioning the garment of your unique mission and path. The substance of your yarn is also woven into the lives of others because you walked with them for a while.

> *Solutions come from where information is integrated from the past, present and future...*
> *A present person is the solution to every problem.*
>
> —Dr. Vernon Woolf, Founder and Director of the International Academy of Holodynamics

It's not possible for me to know where you are regarding your knowledge and understanding of the nature of conflict and its accompanying opportunities and threats. *Transforming Everyday Conflict* is not designed to be a comprehensive tutorial on all aspects of conflict. My focus is to provide a select number of examples of how to communicate responsibly and effectively when certain types of ordinary conflict present themselves in your daily life.

As you study the table of contents you might find one or more of the chapters coming into focus as having the potential to provide an immediate impact on a situation you are experiencing. I suggest you begin with the Introduction, How to Use This Book, and Chapter 1, Three Powerful Keys to Understanding Conflict. Then if Chapter 6 on the art and science of giving directions stands out, read that next. If Chapter 9 on how to deal with another's anger is important to you, skip to that.

Treat the book as a personal reference guide that you can move through or refer to as needed. Get to know it. For more complex conflicts, or at any time you choose, it will be helpful to review the Introduction, How to Use This Book, and Chapter 1 again to renew your expanded understanding of the cause of conflict and the principles involved.

> *To the man who only has a hammer in the toolkit, every problem looks like a nail.*
>
> —Abraham Maslow

Here are just a few ways you can be prepared, practice, and then help others around you acquire the tools and processes in *Transforming Everyday Conflict*:

- If you are experiencing a conflict now or are about to enter a potential conflict with someone, take time to review the strategies. Find the one that is most like the conflict opportunity you are about to experience. Look for ways to speak, listen, and clarify that might be helpful in advancing greater harmony or resolution. Then *apply* what you know!

- In teaching and coaching others in conflict, I often recommend reproducing and downsizing a few copies of these checklists to fit in your day-timer or calendar so they are with you wherever you are. Then if you experience an event, you can quickly take a brief time-out and review some good responses for yourself.

- If you encounter someone else who is distressed, you can easily pull out a checklist and offer it for their consideration. We all feel a little safer when there is structure, orderliness, and even a *to-do* aspect to something new or scary for us. The assistance of knowing how to *do this first, and then do that* can be reassuring until we feel safe enough to move forward, modifying as we go with our own internal guidance. With a simple list on a piece of paper you might open the door to a change of perspective for them!

- If you serve on committees or boards in your place of employment or in your community, consider discussing together how the group will make decisions. You can share some of these processes or checklists with the group, discuss them, and see what might be useful for your group's goals and directives. Then choose and practice together! Evaluate how it works, and don't forget to celebrate your victories together!

- Sometimes these processes are useful for family meetings during which important decisions need to be made and all family members can benefit from shared information and input. They can also strengthen family relationships. Again, evaluate and celebrate!

Chapter 1

Three powerful keys to understanding conflict

*Nothing in life is to be feared.
It is only to be understood.*

—Marie Curie

Have you ever felt that conflict seems so complicated you don't know what to do or where to start? That's a belief system you can change.

As individuals, we would probably define a conflict differently based on our different cultures, values, beliefs, goals, needs, desires, and attitudes. This definition is a good one:

> *A conflict is a disagreement through which those involved perceive a threat to their needs, interests, or concerns.*

This definition suggests dissonance or tension between people. Conflict and tension are both natural phenomena, and they are both catalysts for change and growth. However, they are not synonymous. If you are experiencing tension, it does not necessarily mean that you are in conflict or that conflict will automatically follow.

Tension is new information, and it can stimulate creativity for a greater potential. Think of the exquisite potential of a violin bow drawn across a violin string that is held in place through tension. If the string is loose, there is no tension that can produce a musical sound. And the strands of the bow are also held in place with tension. Between people, *when tension becomes personal, you have conflict.*

What turns change and tension into conflict is what you *think* about them. Whether you think they are good or bad, you are creating your own reality. You can choose to allow conflict to be a messenger bringing new information, and embrace the opportunity to produce something better, or you can resist change and escalate the tension into a tug of war.

What is it we are really protecting during a conflict? Conflict reveals competing interests. It also gives a name to what is going on when fights break out between individuals, families, groups, organizations, and even nations.

Understanding the nature of conflict at its simplest essence, and how to neutralize its causes, helps us set aside the blame game at the very beginning.

These three keys to understanding the nature of conflict will get you started and simplify the process:

1. Conflict results from mismatched expectations. You get into an argument with someone and both of you come away not feeling good about the encounter. Why? You each had thoughts or expectations about what would happen, how it would go, what you might get out of it, and how you would feel about it. Our thoughts constantly manufacture our expectations.

    If you feel disappointed, upset, or even angry about something, then you had an expectation that something different was supposed to happen. The other person might also be upset because what they expected and wanted did not happen.

    What is an expectation? It is a mental or emotional attitude you hold, something that is looked forward to, or a prospect of some future good or profit. A mismatched expectation is one that does not match your mental or emotional attitude. It might feel like a bad or unsuitable match with what you are holding mentally and emotionally within you.

    The value of being aware of your expectations is that if you have identified what is happening within—what you are really thinking and feeling, then...

- » you will create a better opportunity to receive what you want;
- » you will be listening for an idea, new information, or something you have not heard or tried before that meets or expands your expectations;
- » you will actually discover ideas, tools, or strategies that do meet your expectations or are very close and can be adapted to meet your expectations;
- » you will be more aware of what was actually shared or presented to you; and
- » you will be more aware of what you actually experience.

When you find yourself in conflict with others, first ask yourself this question: *What do I expect from this?* Often we do not even know what we want. As the old saying goes, *If you don't know where you want to go, it's pretty hard to get there.* So a large part of effectively managing conflict lies in being clear about what your expectations are. This might require you to engage in some self-reflection. Just as you might ask some clarifying questions of someone else, you can also ask yourself clarifying questions to identify your expectations. Have an inner dialogue to gain greater clarity about what you need or want. Then you can choose to set some simple goals for communicating with that in mind.

The second question to ask is *What does the other person expect?* This can lead to a level of thinking and action that demonstrates your desire to truly understand the other's point of view. Remember, you don't have to agree, just understand. You might *think* you know what the other person expects, but if you *really* want to know, try asking them. You might begin by saying, "I'm feeling a little uncomfortable about our conversation. I wonder if you would be willing to share with me what it is you are expecting or hoping for. And I would also like to share with you what I am expecting. Can we do this?"

If mismatched expectations are the cause of the conflict, *more and better communication* is likely to be an important part of the solution. This kind of inner dialogue with yourself, and then with others, can help you understand and demonstrate these three important keys in avoiding, managing, or resolving ordinary, daily conflict:

» *Talking* is important because it shows involvement.
» *Listening* is very important because it illustrates caring.
» *Asking clarifying questions* is also very important because it demonstrates a desire to truly understand.

When you engage in these communications, you allow yourself and others to participate and contribute without being controlled or needing to control others. You maximize the opportunity for everyone to reach a higher potential. These communication skills can move you and others through mismatched expectations. They are the basic tools in your repertoire of strategies.

> **Note from "Roger":** *That teaching about the cause of all conflict being mismatched expectations? I got it! And it changes just about everything! Many thanks!*

Transforming Everyday Conflict

"Roger" did get it! He caught the *sense of relief* that we can all feel when we understand—actually realize—that conflict is based on mismatched expectations. *I am not bad. The other guy is not bad. We just had different expectations. Now let's talk about them and find a different outcome together.*

2. Conflict escalates when the issue is more important than the relationship. When a conflict occurs in your family, workplace, or friendships, preserving your relationships is probably a priority. When this is the case, ask yourself, *Is my need to be right over this issue worth damaging or losing the relationship? Is my need to express truth as I know it or to uphold a principle or rule that I believe must be upheld worth damaging or losing the relationship?*

   There is no one right answer to either of these questions. The value in asking and answering them is to clarify your own expectations so you can take a different course of action as needed. Ask yourself, *Is the relationship more important to me than the issue? Is there another way for me to manage this? What is the fullest potential or the highest outcome of this circumstance?* If you know what you need or want, and if you know the solution with the fullest potential, you are more likely to attract and create that outcome.

   > **Note from "Sarah":** *Because you shared stories and because you gave examples of dialogue patterns which I never would have thought of, I have stopped forcing myself to accept the lie that "This person/situation doesn't matter." Instead of moving on and regretfully relegating another relationship to ship-*

> *wreck, somehow what you said—I forget exactly how you worded it, but you said something about "the relationship being more important than the issue."—this was like a revelation somehow. I had permission to do what deep inside I felt was the right thing. I'm feeling more and more empowered to be my better self rather than my worst, hopeless self.*

In "Sarah's" story we can see that her first reaction to conflict was to think that she didn't like feeling wrong, so the other person didn't really matter to her anyway because she was not really connected to the other person. Even while Sarah is saying this, she admits that it is a *lie*—that it isn't true that the other person doesn't matter or that they aren't connected, and if she continues to think and feel this way, this is just another "shipwrecked" relationship.

When Sarah got the connection that the relationship might be more important than the issue, being wrong about the issue was no longer such a big deal. It was okay to be wrong about the issue because she could choose to do what she felt deep down was the right thing to do—for the person, for herself, and for the relationship. Her ability to actually *choose to do the right thing* empowered her. And note that her expression of appreciation was in regard to having samples of how the dialogue might go—knowing what to say in the moment.

> **A CHOICE TIP!**
>
> *When you make a choice, you change the future.*
>
> —Deepak Chopra

3. **Peacemaking and healing are not always pain free.** M. Scott Peck teaches in his book *A World Waiting to Be Born: Civility Rediscovered* that two or more people working on something together form an organization of sorts. He writes, "A healthy organization—whether it is a marriage, a family, or a business corporation—is not one with an absence of problems, but one that is actively and effectively addressing or healing its problems... We need to experience pain for our healing and health... Health is an ongoing process, often painful, of an organism becoming the most—the best—it can be."

To expand on Peck's allegory to the human body, sometimes we think of physical pain or inflammation as the disease or the problem itself, when in fact the inflammatory response is the essential part of the body's healing process. We heal because of it, not in spite of it. When you experience a physical injury, the affected area can become inflamed—red and sore to the touch—as blood rushes to that spot bringing with it all the necessary nutrients and ingredients needed to bring about healing. In conflict, inflammation brings new information—something we weren't aware of before, and it rallies our resources to find the potential resolutions. Resisting discomfort or pain at all costs does not serve us, our relationships, organizations, or nations.

Becoming the best we can be is a moment-by-moment encounter no matter where we are, whether we are alone or in a relationship.

Chapter 2

The power of choice

Choices may be unbelievably hard but they're never impossible. To say you have no choice is to release yourself from responsibility and that's not how a person with integrity acts.

—Patrick Ness, *Monsters of Men*

People who perceive themselves as disempowered or victimized usually feel that they have no power, no influence, and no ability to make a difference. And they feel neglected. They think that they are in that circumstance either because something outside of them is controlling them or because they had no other choice. Has this happened to you?

It is the *expansion of choice or the opportunity to decide or influence* that motivates people to go beyond their powerlessness into competence, and then from that sense of competency and confidence into achievement.

The premise behind education, training, and coaching is to assist others in finding their own competencies, tapping in to their own unique resourcefulness and becoming better able to manage the circumstances of their lives.

You can choose!

This is what we can say to ourselves and to others we would assist: *You CAN choose.* We can motivate ourselves and others and offer relief from tension and inner turmoil by providing choices.

For example, you can help children practice contacting their inner potential by providing two choices that are equally safe and allowing them to choose what works best for them. As they grow through their practice of choosing, help them see that there is *always* a choice, that each choice has a consequence, and that sometimes one or more of the choices involves some level of risk. These consequences can guide their subsequent choices.

Alberta Fredricksen

When we routinely create opportunities for choosing, people do not feel so conflicted or deprived when they occasionally encounter situations in which a parent, organization, or employer does not permit choice.

Active participation and involvement in decision-making pushes powerlessness into the background. For instance, even when setting boundaries or disciplines, the individual can be given two or three options and the authority to decide which one to fulfill. If being the decision maker cannot work in a particular circumstance, the act of being able to provide input before the decision is made expands one's sense of choice.

All of us are supervisors at some level—in our families as parents or older siblings, at work, when training a pet, or, most important, when supervising and governing ourselves and our own choices in life. If you are in a supervisory or leadership role in an organization or as an employer, it is important to understand that most people consider *control* to be a supervisory or administrative function. Imposing control is usually acceptable when it can be shown to fit within broad limits set for meeting basic human needs for safety, effective achievement, success, and belonging. However, when people feel that control is being used to enforce compliance, some will resist.

Even though most people do what they are asked if the consequence or the reward is great enough, a conscious or enlightened leader or supervisor seeks to increase cooperation and empower others through *offering opportunity to choose* wisely.

> **A CHOICE TIP!**
>
> *We have two choices: continue to blame the world for our stress or take responsibility for own reactions and deliberately change our emotional climate.*
>
> —Doc Childre and Howard Martin,
> *The HeartMath Solution*

Chapter 3

Seeking and offering forgiveness

Be assured that if you knew all, you would pardon all.

—Thomas à Kempis

Along with choice, forgiveness is a powerful tool for managing and resolving conflict. It can also be loaded with the baggage of our past experiences and expectations.

Memories are stored in our cells as well as in our minds, and they can be triggered repeatedly. Being unwilling to give and receive forgiveness, and holding on to negative feelings, can contribute to physical illness and disease. This cellular memory is something we can choose to be more aware of consciously, day by day and moment by moment. If we cannot or will not forgive, we hold on to our feelings, our emotions, and our stresses, and they can get larger and larger.

A metaphor illustrating this point is that when we hold on to an emotional charge, we are creating a file that goes into a folder. The folder gets thicker with accumulated files (emotional charges). When one of the files gets triggered, the whole folder opens and we find ourselves dealing with multiple situations and multiple emotional charges.

Choosing to forgive is really in your best interest. When you choose to forgive you have the ability to transform what you have been holding into a fuller potential for you and for others involved.

Some of us associate the principle of forgiveness with our spirituality or our religion. We believe God or Spirit has forgiven us and we want that part of Spirit within us to forgive others. Some think it is something we are supposed to do, must do, or are required to do. In other words, we feel that we have no choice. As stated earlier, this can lead to various forms of resistance. The truth is that you do have a choice. Instead of experiencing powerlessness, resistance, or anger, you can choose to shift that perception to what I like to call *enlightened self-interest.*

Forgiveness IS enlightened self-interest

In a truly conscious world, everything and everyone is connected. This connectedness can be described as "heart coherence." The Institute of HeartMath conducts research, teaches coherence, and trains people around the world in how to achieve heart coherence. This explanation of heart coherence comes from their website:

> Coherence, in relation to any system, including the human body, refers to a logical, orderly and harmonious connectedness between parts. Borrowing from physics, when we are in a coherent state, virtually no energy is wasted because our systems are performing optimally and there is synchronization between the heart, respiratory system, blood-pressure rhythms, heart-rate variability patterns, etc. When we speak of heart-rhythm coherence, we are referring to smooth, ordered heart-rhythm patterns. Among the many benefits of coherence are calmness, good energy levels, clear thinking and proper immune-system function.
>
> Each of us is capable of achieving, maintaining and increasing our coherence. One of the simplest and quickest paths to heart coherence is through intentional positive feelings—compassion, caring, love and other such emotions. In contrast, we can quickly become incoherent when we experience negative attitudes such as anger, fear and anxiety. [http://www.heartmath.org/faqs/research/research-faqs.html]

Even the simplest of actions like quieting yourself, placing your hand on your heart, breathing calmly, and intentionally thinking about and experiencing those higher frequencies of appreciation, gratitude, love, compassion, and caring can produce increased coherence quickly.

In the midst of a conflict, the ability to come into greater coherence within your body enhances your ability to bring coherence to the other(s) in the conflict. If you can shift your perception to understanding, and then gratitude or appreciation for another, you can find a fuller potential for resolution.

Choosing to ask for forgiveness or gracefully offering forgiveness when asked for it by someone else enhances heart coherence. Forgiveness is an important tool for surviving and living together in a way that acknowledges our connectedness. It has the potential to transform our future.

How do you begin transforming through forgiveness?

Forgiveness is defined by your management of expectations and behaviors. Let us begin with what forgiveness is not. Forgiveness is not rolling over, giving up, or becoming a doormat. It is not a feeling and it is not forgetting. Forgetting is a passive process in which a matter fades from memory merely with the passing of time.

Forgiving is an act of the will. Sometimes we begin the process of forgiveness with a decision and then we continue by *"faking it until we make it!"* We practice by reaffirming our decision over and over again.

You are making a decision when you choose to forgive someone for having done something to you or to your loved ones that has caused hurt, harm, or stress. Unlike forgetting, forgiving is an active process that has two parts—a conscious choice, and an awakened plan of action. An awakened plan of action includes choosing from a list of specific appropriate behaviors. It works like this:

1. First, choose to forgive. Then when thoughts or feelings reappear about this situation, gently reaffirm your choice. Just as a mature adult might lead a child (the child portion of you who has the feelings of being hurt or of wanting to get even), you can gently remind yourself that you have already chosen to forgive. You can think, *I don't have to revolve this again. I have already decided to forgive this person or this situation.* Gently reaffirm your choice and then choose an appropriate forgiveness behavior.

2. What is an appropriate forgiveness behavior? Once you make the conscious decision to forgive, then you need to know what that forgiveness will look like, sound like, feel like, and be like in the future. Make a list of specific appropriate behaviors that will replace thoughts and feelings that come from revolving the conflict again. Your awakened plan of action can include the following options, as well as others you can create:

    A. Overlook or pardon the harm.

    B. Thank someone for what you have learned or gained through the processing of differences.

    C. Stop talking about the issue to others.

    D. Choose to give up your resentment and acknowledge this repeatedly to yourself or to someone you truly trust. A part of this is to surrender any desire or need to punish or exact a penalty.

E. When you are aware of troubling or resentful thoughts or feelings, snap your fingers or clap your hands. This is a signal to your brain to Stop! Then replace them with thoughts you want to be holding in your conscious awareness.

F. Do not bring the situation up to use against others, or allow it to stand between you or hinder your relationship in the future.

G. Absolve or cancel any sense of debt or obligation someone owes you.

H. Acknowledge any anger you feel and then examine that feeling to discover the new information that will allow you to shift that feeling to a more productive energy.

I. Look for the positive attributes of others and share them.

J. Engage in a heart-centering activity to increase your level of heart coherence.

K. Ask your heart's intelligence to join with your mind's intelligence to show you more options when a conflict arrives in the future.

Seeking Forgiveness and Apologizing

Forgiveness clears the trees that block the Light!

—Unknown

What does it look like, sound like, and feel like when you seek forgiveness from someone else for harm you might have caused them? It requires admitting wrongdoing and being authentically sorry for what you did, said, or set in action. This is repentance.

Following an admission comes the opportunity to restore what has been damaged as much as possible. Seeking forgiveness or apologizing can include your effort to "make whole" that which has been damaged. This is restitution.

Today many court systems are requiring mediation for claimants in small claims courts. Trained volunteer mediators offer their services to help people reach voluntary agreements. One of the primary elements involved in mediation is finding and agreeing on what can be done to make restitution for what has occurred.

Some of the elements of an apology, admission, or confession are:

- Address it to everyone involved.
- Be specific about both your actions and your attitudes about it.
- Avoid using vague or contradictory language like *if*, *but*, and *maybe*.
- Apologize expressing your sorrow or regret.
- Accept the consequences and make restitution.
- Specifically request forgiveness. *Can you or will you forgive me?*
- Whether or not your apology is accepted, alter your behavior by changing your actions and attitudes.

Sorry is a hard word, even though many of us were taught as children to say we were sorry for some misbehavior. We were learning and our parents were teaching what was appropriate. Most of us have a hard time apologizing even when we have come to terms with what we've done that was not right.

Fear is usually at the top of the list of reasons why we don't like to apologize as adults. Perhaps it is like admitting guilt, which can have legal ramifications. Perhaps we have a fear of others piling on if we say we are sorry. Maybe those we have harmed will not believe that we are sorry, and refuse our apology. Then what?

> **A CHOICE TIP!**
>
> *The only person you can be certain of changing is yourself…If your attitude is that everything would be fine if other people changed, you are in a weak, dependent position.*
>
> —Thomas Crum, Aikido Master and author of *The Magic of Conflict: Turning a Life of Work into a Work of Art*

If someone does refuse your apology, there is not much benefit in trying to persuade them. And it doesn't help you or them to try to psychoanalyze why they won't forgive you. Don't be defensive or assess their behavior. One way to respond is to gently say, "I'm very sorry to hear that. And I am genuinely sorry for what I have done. I respect the fact that you can't forgive me now. If you want to talk about this sometime in the future, I am open to that. I hope someday we can move past this." This kind of response maintains your integrity, honors the other's free will, confirms your regret or sorrow again, and leaves the door open for a possible future reconciliation.

Fulfill any opportunities or requirements for restitution. Reaffirm your personal choices to alter your actions and attitudes—and move on! And if spiritual practices are a part of your life, rely on them and pray for forgiveness and a restored sense of peace for all involved.

Some of these ideas might seem too simple for the complexities and magnitude of harm experienced by individuals and groups in the history of our planet. Offering and receiving forgiveness is an intensely personal experience.

Attempting to change others as a solution to conflict does not work. The change we seek to provide relief, respite from painful feelings, and resolution must come from within.

This means that every thought, feeling, word, and action counts. Changing your individual state of consciousness can alter what you attract to your life, and it can change and elevate mankind's collective consciousness. *Forgiveness lets your thoughts pass through effortlessly.*

Sincere forgiveness isn't colored with expectations that the other person apologize or change. Don't worry whether or not they finally understand you. Love them and release them. Life feeds back truth to people in its own way and time—just like it does for you and me.

—Sara Paddison, *The Hidden Power of the Heart*

REFLECTION

Review the list of appropriate forgiveness behaviors above. Add any others that come to your awareness that would work for you. Choose one or two that you will concentrate on applying. Begin today to make all things new within you.

Chapter 4

Seven tips for managing your own history during conflict

Those who don't know history are doomed to repeat it.

—Edmund Burke

Transforming Everyday Conflict

The biggest obstacle to effective conflict management might just be your own history. It has been said that all conflicts have histories that go beyond the current events! You and the others in your relationships all have past histories when it comes to communicating, building relationships, and managing or mismanaging conflict. So as students of history, let us all first learn what we can about ourselves and the conflicts we attract into our lives so that we don't have to repeat them!

Your patterns of behavior are built on your perceptions of what is happening to you and how others are relating to you. And most of us have our own best interests in mind when we are negotiating our way through expectations that are not being met. This colors how we see others and what we project onto them when we sense the contrasts and tangled energies that we call conflict.

The Seven Tips:

1. Remember that people (even you) are rarely as benevolent as they perceive themselves to be. We tend to see our intentions as good, not only for ourselves but for others, too. Just notice how often you have easy reasons (or justifications) for what you do, and are ready, even eager, to explain what you are doing and why you are doing it if you are challenged in some way.

2. Remind yourself that others are rarely as evil as their opponents perceive them to be. Give others the same benefit of the doubt that you expect them to give you. In this way you can hold the intention and a positive energy field so that others have support and opportunity to choose to behave in the best potential way for them and for you.

3. Be aware that people rarely spend as much time thinking about the issues that upset you as you or others think they do. When *you* are experiencing a sense of conflict, others might not even notice because they are not as invested in the issue as you are.

4. Realize that most aspects of conflict spin off other events and are not the result of cold-hearted calculation. Others might not be planning or thinking through what is happening, and they might not even see a need to be seeking common ground.

5. Come from the position that almost all behavior is motivated by positive intention rather than negative intention. Most people do not set out to deliberately hurt someone else or cause upset for others and themselves. And they are often surprised when someone else is offended or put off in some way. At the same time it is true that our positive intentions frequently arise from our instincts to take care of and protect ourselves.

6. Understand how patterns established in previous experiences impact present perceptions. Every conflict has a history that extends beyond the present. We are results of our own histories of relationships with others. If you have experienced hurt or harm in previous relationships, be vigilant not to project similar motivations, intentions, and actions onto others in your current or future relationships.

7. If you have difficulty remembering the first six tips, take a moment to mentally go to "the balcony" to get a better viewpoint of the interactions that you and others are experiencing. Going to the balcony means stepping outside the issue and going to a higher or

elevated position where you can look down on the situation, seeing all the parts at once. You always have the opportunity to choose again, which will change the energy field so that others can also choose again.

A CHOICE TIP!

*Remember, if you don't choose to be offended,
you don't have to fight back!*

—Elizabeth C. Prophet

REFLECTION

Pause here and take a moment to reflect on the seven tips above. Place your hand on your heart and breathe calmly. Then read them again to see which ones create some level of resonance within you. Make a note of those that generate such a response within you and consider adding the positive equivalent to your list of conscious, appropriate forgiveness behaviors from Chapter 3.

Chapter 5

Five mistakes to avoid during conflict

We cannot solve our problems with the same thinking we used when we created them.

—Albert Einstein

There are many positive strategies and processes to use in managing conflict effectively. It is also very important to know the pitfalls and how to avoid them.

You will enhance your success in achieving and maintaining heart peace if you stay aware of the energies that are the indicators and outcomes of conflict. These energies begin with small contrasts that come from mismatched expectations among people. And there are some mistakes you can avoid making if you know about them before the opportunity to make them comes up.

Safely and Effectively Avoid These Five Mistakes during Conflict

1. **Becoming detached** – It can be a mistake to become detached. Stay aware of the energies that are the indicators and outcomes of conflict so you can monitor and track them. Your enhanced awareness allows you to maintain more control in effective ways. And you also really want to have a compassionate concern for both the people and the issues involved. Your engagement and genuine concern can motivate others toward solutions.

2. **"Awfulizing"** – Every conflict has a history that extends beyond the present. "Awfulizing" is the tendency to escalate a situation to its worst-case scenario. One person tries to top the other person's horrible and awful story with one of their own. The goal is to find *common ground* regarding what can be done to resolve problems, not common misery.

3. **Letting conflict establish or alter your agenda** – If you want to be an effective change agent in resolving con-

flict, do the *important* things in the situation and consider delegating the *urgent* things. An effective change agent focuses on good will and common ground, and includes others to take on roles and responsibilities. Do those things that *only you* can do. There will always be distractions and seemingly urgent things that can be done effectively by others rather than by you.

4. **Engaging in power struggles** – There is a significant relationship between *power* and *authority*. Your *authority* increases when you empower others. *Power* tends to be perceived as coercive, while *authority* involves respect. Unless you are prepared to waste time, don't argue. Unless you are prepared to miss the best resolution for the conflict, don't choose to engage in battles. Take full responsibility for your thoughts and feelings. Taking responsibility for others' emotions sets you up to lose in a power struggle.

Being sidetracked by the projections of others – Projection is an emotional release for many people, and sometimes people project their own flaws, weaknesses, and motivations onto others. Avoid accusations and generalizations like *"you people,"* *"everybody says,"* *"they,"* and *"everyone else."* Encourage specific speech and participation so others can speak safely for themselves. There is no need for anyone to be reduced to mind reading.

REFLECTION

Once again, pause and take a moment to reflect on the five mistakes above. Which ones create some level of resonance within you? Make a note of them so you can be more keenly aware of them when they begin to appear in conflicts you are involved in managing for yourself or others.

Chapter 6

The art and science of giving directions

*Directions are instructions given to explain how.
Direction is a vision offered to explain why.*

—Simon Sinek

The purpose of giving directions is to provide clarity and confidence for all participants. It diminishes confusion and provides an organized structure designed to create maximum opportunity for success. Good instructions can also reduce the risk of conflict.

In my forty-plus years as an educator and school administrator, there were thousands of times I observed students and teachers in classrooms, libraries, playgrounds, and cafeterias. I observed many frustrated teachers trying to work with what seemed like unruly students. I noticed when I or other administrative colleagues complained about adult staff members who just couldn't or wouldn't do things as we expected them to do them.

One of the main duties of a teacher is to give directions to students. Teachers do this over and over, all day long. And sadly it is something many teachers have never been taught how to do successfully.

In the summer before I filled the position of elementary school principal, I was blessed with the opportunity to be trained at the UCLA Graduate School of Education, University Elementary School, under the direction of Dr. Madeline C. Hunter. It was there that I learned the most valuable strategy that I was ever taught in my years in education.

That strategy was "The Art and Science of Giving Directions." When I shared this tool with other educators in my school system, I observed those frustrated teachers and those seemingly unruly students have miracle turn-arounds in behavior and productivity. As the teachers and other adults in the schools learned how to give directions effectively, everyone—adults and students—felt more successful! And I must admit that I felt great relief in the principal's office with less traffic for alleged misbehavior!

Previously, when these teachers and adults would begin to speak to give directions, they did so without much thought or planning. The results were often chaotic and unsuccessful. The adults competed with other distractions. Students continued talking or carrying on with other activities while the teacher was trying to deliver directions. Not surprisingly, when asked to perform the directions students did not know what to do. They talked to each other or laughed to avoid appearing like they didn't know what to do, or they raised their hands to repeatedly ask for help. The results were noisy, unproductive class environments and frustrated teachers. The natural reaction is to blame the students for poor behavior and for preventing the teacher from doing a good job, but such blame is misplaced.

Unfortunately these results are not limited to students and teachers in classrooms. This problem can occur whenever someone tries to coordinate or facilitate the efforts of a group of people to achieve a certain goal. The facilitator or leader continues to try to talk over the noise and chaos. People who really want to listen and follow through cannot hear the directions. The only options are to keep asking for the directions over and over again or to give up trying to do the task. The results are haphazard or unacceptable, and the goal is not accomplished in the time available.

All of us who routinely work with others can benefit from learning how to effectively give directions. I cannot begin to count the number of times I have been able to share this one tool that can improve communication, eliminate confusion, and give everyone the maximum opportunity to be successful.

If you are facilitating the work of others and there seems to be confusion, before you blame others for not listening well, look to yourself. *How well did you plan and deliver the directions?* You have the power to ensure greater success through effective planning and implementation!

The Art and Science of Giving Directions
[Adapted from Dr. Madeline C. Hunter's Teacher Training, UCLA, School of Education, Los Angeles, California]

There are two main sections to this process: *planning* the directions, and *implementing* the directions. The planning is just as important as the delivery.

As a group leader, teacher, or facilitator, if you carefully plan and practice implementing this tool, you will not always have to do it so precisely; it will become a habit for you and for your group. If something does not go as expected, don't be quick to blame the group. First check to see how effectively you delivered the directions. Students, and people in general, want to do well and be successful. Give them the best start and you will all be happy!

Planning

How many?

- General rule: Never give more than *three* directions at one time, even to adults.

- Give only one *new* direction in a set of directions. (This means that the other two directions are activities everyone has practiced and done before successfully.)

Sequence

- Give the directions in the order they are to be followed. (Auditorily in order.)
- Use your fingers to make it graphic. Hold up one, then two, then three fingers. (Visually in order as you speak them.)

Written or oral?

- Use both written and oral directions when practical and appropriate.
- Use written directions when directions are long or complicated.
- Use written directions when people are working alone on the assignment.
- When the same directions must be given often, post written directions in a visible place. This allows for the leader to quietly point or direct someone individually to the directions instead of creating a distraction by giving them again.
- You can also prepare a written handout to distribute so participants can review the directions at their seat or workspace without moving about.
- Sometimes it is useful to model the directions so they can see you performing them.

Timing

- Give directions just before the activity is to be performed. Leaving time between giving directions and carrying them out leaves more room for confusion and diminishes success.

Individualizing

- Some people need extra assistance. Move about and see how participants are doing with the task. Help them quietly and individually at their workspace. You can also ask them to raise a hand if they need help so that you can come to them.

Implementation

Attention

- Use a signal to get everyone's attention before giving group directions. Don't compete with a distraction.

- Signals can be blinking lights, a bell or chime, a verbal cue such as "My turn," or clapping your hands in a particular rhythm. If the room is noisy with planned activity, you can also hold your arm up high with the instruction that everyone who sees you immediately holds their arm up high until all have seen and quieted down to receive your next instruction.

Give directions

- Give directions in a way that reflects your conscious, thoughtful, and sequential planning.

Check for understanding

- Always get feedback from the person or group to confirm they know what the directions are before signaling their release to begin work. An example might be to ask, "How many steps were there in the directions? What was the first one? What was the second one?"

- If there is confusion, repeat the directions using verbal and visual signals. Check for understanding again.

- Model the directions again if appropriate.
- Remind participants to wait for the signal to begin before starting the work so that they don't begin moving around while others do not yet understand what to do.

Translate to action

- Instruct participants that they are not to begin work until you give the signal.
- Give a signal to release them to begin to perform the directions. This can be as simple as "Go."

Remediate

- Re-teach the directions as needed or for only those individuals who need it.
- Monitor and check to see if there are those who need help as they are working or who may have started well but have forgotten next steps.

As a weak and potentially confusing example, visualize a leader giving directions to a group of ten volunteering adults who are responsible for transporting supplies to elderly recipients around your city who are confined to their homes. The leader says, "Remember to knock on the doors or ring the bell before you go in. The people inside are sometimes startled if you just walk in. Now, it's important to talk a little with them and not just drop off the supplies and leave, but don't stay long because you have to get all your boxes delivered. But before we leave here, we need to check to make sure we have correct addresses—and oh yeah, we have to double-check the names to make sure we haven't left anyone off the list. So get your list from the office staff and then go through the boxes you are delivering to see that the correct supplies are in

Transforming Everyday Conflict

the boxes. Okay, let's get started. We don't want to be late on these deliveries."

Considering what you've learned in this chapter, let's look at how the leader might plan the directions in advance and prepare a handout for each volunteer to take with them. All the volunteers are gathered at the assigned time. The leader invites the volunteers to be seated as she distributes and talks through the directions with them. She says:

> Our secretary has prepared a list of the names, addresses, and specific supplies that each one of you is expected to deliver today. Each one of you will have five deliveries to make. Your specific list of recipients is stapled to this direction sheet.
>
> Please look now to make sure that your name is at the top of your list of recipients. Is there anyone who does not have a list with your own name at the top? Raise your hand if your name is not at the top of your list. (Wait and check for understanding.)
>
> Please review the addresses on your list. Raise your hand if there are any addresses that you do not know how to locate. (Wait and check for understanding.)
>
> Before we leave here, there are three (3) directions for you to complete.
>
>> Number one [raising one finger]: Locate the five boxes that are labeled with the names of your recipients.
>>
>> Number two [raising two fingers]: Open each box and check off the supplies that are supposed to go to each recipient. If any box is missing something, tell the secretary and she will get that item for the box.

Number three [raising three fingers]: When all your boxes are complete, load them into your vehicle and return here for final instructions.

Okay, how many directions were there? (Yes, three.)

Who will tell us the first direction? [Choose someone to repeat it and then ask, "Who agrees? Anyone disagree?"]

Who will tell us the second direction? [Repeat as above]

And what is the third direction? [Repeat as above]

Good. Now complete these three directions and return here. [When everyone has checked their boxes, loaded them into their vehicles, and returned, then continue with the written direction sheet.]

Let's go over the directions on How to Greet and Talk with Recipients.

Number one, always ring the bell or knock on the door to gain permission to enter. If no one answers or you feel something is not right, use your cell phone to call the secretary [telephone number here]. She will give you further instructions.

Number two, greet the recipient. Be friendly. Smile. Deposit your box of supplies on a table or somewhere easy and safe for them to unpack it, and leave within approximately five minutes in order to have time to deliver all five boxes within our scheduled time frame.

Number three, when you have completed five deliveries, call the secretary [telephone number here] and report that you are complete. Then you are free to go.

[Ask for questions and when everyone is set, thank them for volunteering their time and service. Send them on their way with a smile, a "Be safe," and another "Thank You."]

REFLECTION

This tool is a real team builder and I strongly recommend that you adopt it and find ways to pay it forward! Reduce it in size and carry copies of it with you to give to someone who might need it. Those who receive this kind of support get to experience success. And their gratitude is a great reward for being prepared to help someone achieve cooperation and complete goals in a timely way!

FREE GIFT!

As a special bonus for you as readers of this book who are demonstrating your desire and willingness to create more responsible and effective communication and stronger relationships, I want to offer another roadmap—a checklist for assessing conflict within groups or organizations. You may access this complimentary document at this link: http://www.heartpeacenow.com/conflict-assessment-checklist.html

Chapter 7

Basic steps for problem-solving

*The problem is not that there are problems.
The problem is expecting otherwise and thinking
that having problems is a problem.*

—Theodore Rubin

Thinking that having a problem is a problem is a set-up to believing that a problem is equal to conflict. Solutions that come from effective problem-solving are the gifts that come from working with others.

Cooperative problem-solving offers the greatest opportunity for substantial gains in the quality of relationships, innovative solutions, and commitment to action. It can sometimes be time-consuming, and therefore it's not practical in all instances, but sometimes problem-solving can be the best mode of conflict management.

Basic Key Steps

- **Recognize that a problem exists.** If the problem is between two individuals, both agree to meet together and set a time and place. If the problem involves others, leaders or facilitators who realize that there is a problem come together to acknowledge the problem and embark on problem-solving, including the appropriate steps below.

- **Involve the key people** affected by the problem. It's important that those who are affected by the problem are invited or have some level of representation in the group coming together to solve it.

- **Define the problem.** One person can do this to begin a discussion and then the other people involved can add to it until you have a definition that appropriately identifies the issue for all.

- **Describe** the separate aspects of the overall issue; give your viewpoint; and when appropriate, share how the *behavior* impacts you and your *feelings*. Each person involved needs to have an equitable amount of time to do the same from their viewpoint.

- **Actively listen** to understand the other's point of view. *Ask clarifying questions* as needed.
- **Clarify** each person's perception of the problem. This is also a *checking for understanding* to know how each one perceives the situation. This usually begins to clarify things and a solution might begin to emerge.
- If a problem still exists, **summarize the needs** of each person and ask for agreement to move into the problem-solving steps below.

Problem-Solving Steps

- **Brainstorm.** Everyone contributes to generating possible solutions. Write all of them down without critiquing any of them. This is not the time to point out why something suggested won't work. Just capture all the suggestions on paper or a whiteboard where everyone can see them.
- **Establish criteria needed for a good solution.** These are the things that are necessary for a solution that works to solve the problem.
- **Evaluate each of the suggested solutions** that were generated during the brainstorming. Apply the criteria for a good solution to each idea to estimate the probability of reaching the desired needs or outcomes. Eliminate the ideas that don't meet the criteria. Identify the potential ideas for solution.
- **Choose one solution.** This can be accomplished by simple voting. Beware of creating winners and losers. Work for consensus if possible. Review the Fist to Five process in Chapter 13. If no acceptable solution arises, go back to summarizing the needs and refining the criteria for assessment, and start these steps again with brainstorming to select another potential solution.

- Develop an action plan and implement the solution (who, what, where, when, and resources needed). See Appendix A for a sample.

- Set a time to **evaluate the outcomes of the implemented solution.**

REFLECTION

This process can be adapted to problem-solve between two individuals or within a family, organization, or community. Your creativity is essential! And remember that anyone else who is a party to the situation has creativity, too. Be alert and welcoming to creativity from any source!

Chapter 8

How to make tough decisions

The doors we open and close each day decide the lives we live.

—Flora Whittemore

Our lives are composed of billions and quadrillions of decisions. The number of decisions in a full life span might not even be calculable. We make decisions all the time and usually we are completely unaware that we are making them. They are routine. What will I eat for breakfast? Should I gas up the car today or tomorrow? Shall I take the stairs or the elevator today? Will I pick up the mail now or in a couple of hours? Do I want the blue one or the green one?

When we encounter a little tension, friction, or push-pull energy, it adds a level of difficulty to making decisions. That's when we can begin to think that we are experiencing conflict. Somehow just the presence of the word *conflict* makes us more aware that there could be consequences to our choice that might impact us or others. It's very important to know that a good decision for you might not be a good decision for me. And what is a very hard decision for me might be simple for you.

Each of us is the result of all that has gone before in our lives. So knowing how to make tough decisions is very personal and needs to be personalized—by you! Take what is offered here as a guide and then make it your own by personalizing it for each decision you need to make as it appears in your life. This process will not always be the same. Be free enough to alter it. Be creative! The choice is yours!

The Process

When you have a tough decision to make, consider these suggestions for reducing stress and exercising your choices in decision-making.

Alberta Fredricksen

1. Be aware that you can't control the outcome of a decision or the responses of others to your decision. All you can do is control the decision-making process for you.

2. Start the process by identifying your wants and needs. Jot them down on paper even if they seem contradictory.

3. Rank the things you want and need. If you find contradictory needs, ask yourself, *Which would I choose?* Example: When you are seeking a new job, do you prefer a high salary or creative freedom? Do you want to live in a large city or a smaller community? What does your family need to thrive best?

4. Gather all the information necessary to make that decision. Look at alternatives, consequences, advantages, and disadvantages. Don't let your emotions interfere with this process. Be as objective as possible.

5. After you have been as objective as possible, consider and visualize how you would *feel* after you select each option on your list. Reflect and factor in how important what you *feel* really is to you.

6. Determine how much of a risk you're willing to take. Then consider these potential strategies:

    A. Choose the safest option—the one that cannot fail.

    B. Pick the option with the best odds for success.

    C. Select the option with the most desirable outcome despite the risk.

    D. Identify any other options that arise during this process and consider them fully.

7. Identify any option you could not live with if it failed. Eliminate any option that might result in a loss you won't be able to live with despite the high odds for the option's success.

8. Plan for how you would deal with any negative consequences of your choice.

9. If appropriate, use the sample action plan in Appendix A to capture your decisions.

> **A CHOICE TIP!**
>
> *Crying is all right in its way while it lasts. But you have to stop sooner or later, and then you still have to decide what to do.*
>
> —C.S. Lewis, *The Silver Chair*

REFLECTION

Recall a difficult decision you had to make in the past that turned out very successfully for you. Think through all the details of how you came to that decision. Did you do research? Talk with trusted family or friends? Consult an expert? Make a list of alternatives? Experiment with one or two choices? Make notes of whatever you did (or did not do) that worked. Capture the steps you took to get there. Based on your own assessment of past successful experiences, develop your own criteria for making hard decisions. Consider adding to it or incorporate it into the one provided in this chapter.

Chapter 9

How to deal with another's anger

There are two things a person should never be angry at, what they can help, and what they cannot.

—Plato

Anger is a reactive emotion. The danger comes when we choose to respond to another person's anger, whether or not we caused it, by getting hooked into an angry response ourselves. We can choose to view the anger as negative energy that got dumped on us, just as ocean waves in a storm dump their energy on the beach. If we view another's anger as threatening and we react with anger, we have then only added our own anger to deal with as well. Two angry people can accelerate ordinary conflict into a potentially dangerous situation.

> **Note from "Steve":** *I get so angry during conflict. All I want to do is blame the other guy! Somebody told me once that anger is a "secondary emotion"... that the primary cause for stuff is underneath the anger. Since taking your instruction, I have been thinking about that a lot since you really listen to me and kind of mirror what I'm saying/feeling. Now I'm thinking maybe I'm feeling fear and inadequacy so I cover it with anger because I just don't know what to do with the other feelings. This is as far as I've gotten with it but I'm hoping you can help me.*

"Steve" is sharing with us a common feeling of confusion. Anger, fear, feeling inadequate, and sensing loss—all of these emotions are part of a pattern that begins to reveal itself when we sense separation from our connectedness. Some might say this begins when we first start to sense our separation from divinity or God. When we sense separation, we often fall unconsciously into a pattern of emotional reactions. The pattern goes something like this:

- Things are going along as we are used to them being. We are relatively comfortable with the status quo even if it's not good.

- Something happens that rings some kind of alarm that makes us not trust what's happening. Something is different, and we don't know what it is, what it wants, or why it is showing up. So we experience a *loss of trust*.

- When we can't trust what's happening or about to happen, fear makes its appearance—fear of not being able to handle changes, fear of what will be next, *and fear of loss*.

- Once we are fearful, we give room for *doubt*—doubt of others, doubt of God, doubt that we will be okay, doubt that anyone knows or cares where we are or what's happening to us.

- These thoughts, fears, and doubts have now allowed fertile ground for *anger* to appear—*anger over the separation from others*. But what are we angry about? Who is our anger directed to? It is the sense of separation that sets the pattern in motion.

There are a variety of reasons for the loss of trust that heads up this pattern. And depending on the relationship we have with the person we have lost trust in, the intensity is different from situation to situation.

This is the moment to shift your perspective

Movement requires energy. The energy needed to move in a positive direction comes from the emotions we generate when we care enough to get involved. Anger is a form of energy, and it can create movement. The problem is that it doesn't make anyone who receives it or witnesses it or engages in it feel very good. It is the tail end of the pattern that begins with loss of trust.

Even people not involved in a dispute who witness the angry tirade of one person toward another walk away thinking, *"Well, at least I'm not as bad as that guy is. He's a jerk! I wouldn't put up with that from him."* Well, what *would* this person do? When we find it convenient to sit in judgment of the person who lost his temper, we're setting ourselves up to sound superior. The truth is *we* also feel loss of trust when we witness such an angry outburst. And so the pattern begins for us, too. It's a setup for everyone! One person has lost control and unleashed a spiral of negative energy that they will probably feel regret, shame, or guilt about later. The person the anger was directed at will probably feel put down, shamed, embarrassed, fearful, or angry enough to plot some sort of revenge or experience a serious loss of self worth. And the individual who witnessed it will feel fear inside that it could happen to them; outwardly they portray that they are superior and judgmental, and actually unleash their own negative thoughts and words that hold the same angry vibration, though at a softer volume than the one who lost their temper. There is no winner. Everyone loses.

Anger really does not serve anyone well, especially the person giving it voice. It can cause real damage to your physical body. In a cartoon, when a character gets angry, steam comes out of their ears, red creeps over their body from head to toe, and there might even be an explosion or two. The response varies from person to person, but some symptoms include teeth-grinding, fist-clenching, flushing, paling, prickly sensations, numbness, sweating, muscle tension, and temperature changes.

Dr. Mercola, a physician with a prominent internet business and following, states in his article "Risk for Heart Attack or Stroke Increases after Anger Outburst," "A new systematic review involving data on 5,000 heart attacks, 800 strokes, and 300 cases of arrhythmia revealed that not only does anger increase your risk of heart attack, arrhythmia, and stroke, but the risk also rises with frequent anger episodes." [http://articles.mercola.com/sites/articles/archive/2014/03/20/anger-heart-attack-risk.aspx]

Choosing to regularly vent your anger is not healthy for you. And for others it creates fear, dread, an anger response, hostility, and even the avoidance of being in relationship with you because of the probability of being subjected to angry outbursts. Since we are all connected and we seek right relationship with all around us, the loss of relationship is a big price to pay for anger. Loss of relationship carried to extremes explains why there is so much war on planet Earth!

It's much like the fight-or-flight response. Your body thinks it's gearing up for a fight to survive a wrong that's been perpetrated against you. In the brain, the amygdala—the part of the brain that deals with emotion—is firing. It wants to do something, and the time between a trigger event and the amygdala's response can be a quarter of a second. Really! That gives new meaning to the concept of making a snap judgment to be angry.

At the same time, blood flow is increasing to the frontal lobe—specifically the part of the brain that's over the left eye. This area controls reasoning, and is probably what's keeping you from throwing something at someone. The neurological response to anger lasts less than two seconds, which is why the common-sense advice of our grandparents' era still holds up: Wait—and always count to ten when angry before acting or reacting.

Doing the same thing over and over again and expecting a different outcome has been put forth as one of the definitions of insanity. In other words, it does not work.

Someone I know experienced a momentum of angry outbursts when he repeatedly gave counsel and advice to a family member and they didn't follow it. It's a long-established family pattern, and his frustration with not feeling heard and respected, and with having to continue to witness negative outcomes for the other family member for not listening, reduced him to venting his anger regularly and then feeling hopeless about giving in to anger even when nothing changed. He agrees that the anger has changed nothing for the good. And it has probably cost quite a lot in terms of loss of peace of mind for both people, and loss of spiritual energy, too.

This kind of episode fits the old adage that insanity is doing the same thing over and over again and expecting a different outcome. Anger can cause fear, resentment, and apprehension in the one receiving it, and it can cause guilt, shame, and regret in the one delivering it. The bottom line is that *it doesn't work!*

To reduce the anger of another to a level at which both of you can listen, actually hear one another, and then work to solve or resolve the problem, try these tips:

Tips for Dealing with Another's Anger

- **Acknowledge the other person's feelings.** To ignore or pretend you are not noticing another's anger usually makes things worse or accelerates their need to get your attention. Let them know that you can see or hear that they are upset. You might say, "I can see that you are very frustrated."

- **Be aware of your own tenseness or reaction.** Their anger might create a fight-or-flight response in you. Avoid communicating in a way that could result in more distortion of emotion for the angry person. Do not lash back.

- **Use good listening skills and express your willingness to try to solve the problem.** You might say, "I want to hear what you have to say. (I may have made a mistake.) Help me understand. I would like for us to work this out. Other people have been in a situation like this and it worked out okay. We can do it, too."

- **Clarify with some gentle questioning.** Give feedback and request specific feedback from them. Remember that conflict is a result of mismatched expectations, so check on what they were expecting. Reflect on what you were expecting. Share these expectations with one another. This can help both of you clarify what each of you can do to solve the issue or meet on common expectations.

- **Acknowledge a mistake, express regret, and apologize** if the situation calls for it.

- **Determine a course of action.** Explore what can or cannot be done. Plan together how similar situations will be dealt with in the future.

- **Summarize and close.** Communicate what each of you understands about what will happen next or in the future. If needed, you might choose to create a summary memorandum, as shown in the sample in Appendix B.
- **Acknowledge the importance of the relationship** between you, if that is appropriate. Acknowledge that you now have a different understanding as a result of being able to talk together and communicate authentically.

> **A CHOICE TIP!**
>
> *There is always a split second just before you lose your temper when you know you can still stop. You know you have a choice—not to unleash this anger—or to let it loose. Pay attention to this messenger—stop—breathe—wait a couple of moments—put your hand on your heart—come into a greater awareness of heart coherence.*
>
> *Then choose:*
>
> 1. *You can excuse yourself and suggest postponing the conversation to another time and place.*
>
> 2. *If you feel you have regained a level of stability and a sense of heart coherence, you can choose to continue by acknowledging that this does not seem to be going as either one of you expected or hoped. You can then ask to begin a new conversation with each one sharing what they were expecting. (Review the section on mismatched expectations as a cause for conflict, the first key to understanding the nature of conflict described in Chapter 1.)*

REFLECTION

It's not surprising that the word anger is just one letter away from *danger*. It is important to realize that anger is just one emotion in a pattern that is at work within both of you (or all of you). Recognition of the presence of anger can also lead to satisfaction when dealt with appropriately.

> *At the core of all anger is a need that is not being fulfilled.*
>
> —Marshall B. Rosenberg

A CHOICE TIP!

Chapter 10

The art of listening

*Most people do not listen with the intent to understand;
they listen with the intent to reply.*

—Stephen R. Covey,
The 7 Habits of Highly Effective People

A good listener can resolve and even prevent conflict! Even the best of relationships experience some conflict. And the tension it brings is opportunity knocking at the door.

You can actually learn more by listening than you can by talking! When you are experiencing contrast or conflict with others, it might mean that you are trying your best to persuade them of your point of view. And that means you just keep talking—hoping the others will eventually see the light of your position.

Even when someone else is talking, it is very common for us as listeners to be thinking about what we will say next. We can hardly wait for our opportunity to speak again.

We can train ourselves to really listen and try to hear and understand what the speaker is saying. What happens if you shift your strategy and start listening—*really* listening?

> *It is the work of an educated mind to be able to entertain a thought without accepting it.*
>
> —Aristotle

You don't have to agree with a speaker to be an attentive listener. The key is that you demonstrate caring—caring enough to listen to another and genuinely attempting to understand the point of view they express.

Remember that everyone wants to be heard and understood. It is very helpful to be able to model what we hope to receive in return. There are many benefits for us if we learn and demonstrate good listening skills to enhance understanding and thereby bypass or resolve conflict.

Being an active listener is really an extension of The Golden Rule.

To know how to listen to someone else, think about how you would want to be listened to. Listening is not the same as agreeing or feeling a need to do or carry out what is being said. You are there to show that you care enough to really listen. You might ask some clarifying questions to assist the speaker in getting clarity for themselves.

Some of these ideas are intuitive while you listen carefully. For some it might take some practice to develop the skills. Here are some tips for good listeners to know and follow:

1. **Face the speaker.** Sit up straight or lean forward slightly to show your attentiveness through body language.

2. **Maintain eye contact** while also assuring that everyone is comfortably positioned. (There are some cultures in which eye contact is considered impolite or even rude and challenging. Be conscious of who you are with and what the culture is.)

3. **Minimize external distractions.** Turn off the TV, cell phone, and any other distractions. Put down your book or magazine. Ask the speaker and other listeners to do the same.

4. **Respond appropriately** to show that you understand. Murmur ("uh-huh" and "um-hmm") and nod. Raise your eyebrows. Say things such as "Really," "Interesting," and more direct prompts like "What did you do then?" and "What did she say?"

5. **Focus on what the speaker is saying.** Try not to think about what you are going to say next. The conversation will follow a logical flow after the speaker makes

their point. If there is an important point you need to ask about or make comment on, do not interrupt. Instead, make a quick written note so you can remember later at an appropriate point.

6. **Minimize internal distractions.** If your own thoughts keep intruding, simply gently let them go and continue to refocus your attention on the speaker.

7. **Keep an open mind.** Wait until the speaker is finished before speaking unless they ask you a question. Remember that you don't have to agree or disagree with what is being said. Try not to make assumptions about what the speaker is thinking.

8. **Avoid volunteering to the speaker how you have handled a similar situation unless asked.** Unless they specifically ask for advice, assume they just need to talk it out. Offering advice without being asked first is tricky territory. If they follow your advice and the situation turns out badly, it's easy to make it your fault. Your job is to help empower people to make good decisions, look at options, evaluate, choose, live with the choices they made, reevaluate, and take next steps. You are there to support them while they reach their own next steps.

9. **Even if the speaker is launching a complaint against you, wait until they finish before moving to defend yourself.** By doing so, the speaker will feel as though their point has been made, and hopefully they will feel as if they have been heard by you. They won't feel the need to repeat it or talk over you. And you'll know the whole argument before you respond. Generally, on average, we can hear four times faster than we can talk, so we have the ability to sort ideas as they come in and be ready for more. If a lot of information is being giv-

en, take notes while someone else speaks so that you don't interrupt until it is your turn to speak. Then you can use your notes to respond.

10. **Show that you are engaged in the discussion.** Ask questions for clarification, but, once again, wait until the speaker has finished. That way you won't interrupt their train of thought. After you ask questions, paraphrase their point to make sure you didn't misunderstand. You can say things like "So you're saying...," and "Let me see if I understand your reasons for...".

Asking clarifying questions plays an important and positive role in being a good listener.

It's easier to ask and answer questions that have to do with *who, what, where, how,* and *when*: "Can you say more about that?" "How did this work out?" "What other steps did you consider?" "Was this happening before _____ or after the conclusion of _____?" "Who were the others participating in your experiment?" "Where did you complete these steps?"

Questions that begin with the word *why* can be more problematic. *Why* feels more like a personal challenge—a potential threat that might result in a loss of some kind: "Why did you do that?" "Why did you pay that price?" "Why didn't you call me?" "Why would you think that was a good idea?"

You can see how use of the word *why* can initiate that pattern of emotional reactions that lead to anger discussed in Chapter 9.

It is good to be aware that the word *why* raises a level of defensiveness in us. We are more comfortable with *who, what, where, how,* and *when*. Watch your own reactions when questions are asked of you. Be aware of your human personality and the defensiveness you might feel when asked *why*.

Nine Benefits of Being a Good Listener

1. You actually learn more when you listen than when you speak!

2. Listening says to the other person that they are important and you will take the time to hear them. Listening affirms others and contributes to their sense of self-esteem and well-being.

3. Your silence while listening can enhance your understanding of the problem and of others' perspectives.

4. Listening gives you more information that you can use in identifying potential options and making decisions.

5. Listening allows you to be more aware of different perspectives and find an opening for collaborative efforts.

6. Listening doesn't cost you any money. It only takes a little time that is well invested in achieving your goals and building cooperative relationships.

7. You can implement the listening tool by simply choosing to do it. You don't have to enroll in another training program.

8. Listening helps resolve conflict. Listening builds stronger relationships.

9. Talking shows involvement; listening shows caring; and asking clarifying questions shows your desire to better understand what others are thinking, feeling, and saying.

More Tips!

Listening makes our loved ones feel worthy, appreciated, interesting, and respected. Ordinary conversations evolve to a deeper level, as do our relationships. When we listen, we foster the skill in others by acting as a model for positive and effective communication.

In our love relationships, greater communication brings greater intimacy. Parents who really listen to their kids help build their kids' self-esteem. In the business world, listening saves time and money by preventing misunderstandings. And we always learn more when we listen than when we talk.

Listening skills enhance our social, emotional, and professional success, and listening is a skill we can learn.

As you work on developing your listening skills, you might feel a bit panicky when there is a natural pause in the conversation. What should you say next? Learn to settle into the silence and use it to better understand all points of view.

As your listening skills improve, so will your ability to simply be in conversation with others. When clients have complimented my conversational skills, I thought back and noted that I really did not say much. What I did do was listen to that person for quite a long time. I was *present* with them. To really be heard is often the most important part of empowering others to choose next steps for themselves. Many people just need a good sounding board—a safe place to think out loud.

> **Note from "Karen":** *The way I process issues is to talk out loud and hear myself think. But it doesn't*

work if I am by myself. That's what I like about talking to you. You really listen and let me process for myself.

This works in managing conflict, too. I have observed people who, once they had their say on a matter, determined that it really wasn't such a big deal after all, and they might just say something like "I think I know how to move forward with this now, and thanks for listening. I guess that's what I really needed after all."

Chapter 11

How to give information

*The improvement of understanding is for two ends:
first, our own increase of knowledge; secondly,
to enable us to deliver that knowledge to others.*

—John Locke

All of us give and receive information on a daily basis. Consider who you really listen well to and who you tend to tune out. Tuning others out means you can miss important information that you are responsible to know or to convey to others. It can certainly produce conflict, and sometimes lead to an unsafe environment. Caring enough about how others perceive the information you share with them is similar to giving good directions (covered in Chapter 6). A key element is planning how to give information to others.

Key Tips for Sharing Information without Providing Opportunity for Q & A

- **Have a clear idea of what you want** others to understand. Plan what you want to share in advance. As needed, consult Chapter 6 on the art and science of giving directions.

- **Develop a clear message.** Make it brief, aimed at one purpose, congruent, and sequential if needed. Words, body language, touch, and gestures should all support the same message.

- **Choose the right environment.** Make sure you have your listeners' full attention. Choose the right time and place and make sure there are no distractions.

- **Be aware of sender problems.** Be alert to your own assumptions, values, and perceptions, and how these affect the understanding of those who need the information you are relaying.

- **Prepare for the listener.** Think in terms of those listening to your message. What are the potential misunderstandings? How do the listeners usually react to things? Is the information new to those hearing it? Do they need a handout or should the information also be on a whiteboard? Will the information be potentially upsetting? Do you need any other supports for delivering this information?

- **Be responsible for your own thoughts.** Don't necessarily state everything as fact or accepted common knowledge. Be prepared to say things like "I think..." and "It is my opinion...".

- **Describe behavior.** Report *specific, observable actions* without making accusations or generalizations about motives or personality.

- **Describe feelings** by using words that specifically *describe emotions*. "I feel...," "I was disillusioned...," or "I expected...".

- **State your intentions or the outcomes you want.** "I would like..." or "What is needed to move forward is...".

- **Get feedback. Check for understanding. Ask questions.** Listeners might hear you but have an understanding quite different from the one you intend. Don't conclude your presentation until you are certain you have been understood and that those listening know what they are to do next. As needed, give the information or portions of the information again, and then check once more for understanding.

> **A CHOICE TIP!**
>
> *Leaders live by choice, not by accident.*
>
> —Mark Gorman

CHAPTER 12

Handling complaints

Complaints drain joy.

—Toba Beta, *Master of Stupidity*

All of us are recipients of complaints from time to time. They can be from friends or family or they can take place in workplaces or community settings. Be open to hearing them, and don't react like they are somehow wrong. It's just someone conveying new information and seeking some level of resolution.

Acknowledge

- Let the person know you are attending to them verbally and non-verbally.

Use good listening skills

- Allow the person to release pent-up anxieties and/or resentments and calm down.
- Ignore rudeness.
- Don't lecture.
- Don't aggravate by blaming others.
- Don't justify or defend.
- Understand what the experience means to the person. Understanding does not mean acceptance of fault or agreement.

Diagnose the situation

- Use clarifying questions and comments to shed light on the situation.
- Ask questions that convey sincerity and interest, not superiority.
- Make sure you get the necessary details. Ask questions like "How many times did you write to us before you got an answer?" and "Who responded to you?"

Determine a course of action

- If appropriate, give information on your action plan and/or what you can do together to resolve the issue.

Next steps

- If you have made a mistake, or your department has been responsible for a mistake, it is better to admit it than to argue or become defensive.
- Advise the person, "What you are telling me is important for us to know. Thank you for telling me. I am sorry for any upset this has caused you."

Summarize and close

- Summarize the proposed action to ensure mutual understanding of what will happen next and who will do what.
- Verify that you both have the same understanding.
- Write a summary memorandum, as needed, to send after your interaction. See a sample in Appendix B.

Follow up

- Record the details.
- Check the completed agreement.
- Notify your supervisor or anyone else who needs to know about the agreement.

REFLECTION

The life I touch for good or ill will touch another life and that in turn another, until who knows where the trembling stops or in what far place my touch will be felt.

—Frederick Buechner

Chapter 13

Fist to five process for consensus-building

A genuine leader is not a searcher for consensus but a molder of consensus.

—Martin Luther King, Jr.

"Fist to Five" is a tool for gauging support for a proposal or idea in groups. It can help in deciding whether or not to move all the way through consensus-based decision-making. Consensus decision-making in groups is highly desired because you are gaining buy-in from more people. It is also the most time-consuming type of decision-making to achieve.

Fist to Five is a great strategy when you are problem-solving or brainstorming with a group of people. Two key elements to consider are making sure that everyone in the group has the opportunity to speak and offer ideas, and that everyone has a chance to ask questions.

Most groups don't have difficulty beginning discussions. This tool is most valuable when the conversation has gone on long enough and the group now needs a little more structure and direction before moving toward action planning.

Voting creates winners and losers

Don't take a vote too soon. When groups, especially boards or committees who are decision makers, discuss an item on an agenda, there is sometimes a point at which it becomes obvious that if a vote were taken one group would prevail. People are often in a hurry to simply get it done. If someone quickly and prematurely makes a motion and a vote is taken, the net result can be that you now have winners and losers.

This is when you can build stronger relationships. If you employ the Fist to Five strategy, you might be able to turn a divided decision into a consensus so that everyone buys-in to the decision and everyone feels like a winner.

Alberta Fredricksen

The best part of this strategy is that it specifically allows those who have not completely bought-in to the idea to be heard. Even if there is only one person holding back, it might be that this one individual is the only one who realizes why the group's idea or plan might fail. Actively pursuing what might be holding this person back is a demonstration of trying to understand. Allow them to speak about what they are thinking. Ask clarifying questions. After all, the group is responsible for exploring anything that might result in investing time, money, or reputation in pursuit of a plan that might ultimately end in failure.

Fist to Five Strategy for Gauging Support for Ideas and Proposals

[Adapted from the Fist to Five Voting and Consensus tool presented at a workshop for the Kansas State Department of Education, Students Support Services, Boots Adams Alumni Center, University of Kansas, Lawrence, Kansas. See the document describing the Fist to Five process in detail at: http://www.nasco.coop/resources/fist-to-five-voting.]

Fist to Five has the elements of consensus built in and can prepare groups to transition into true consensus if they wish. Most people are accustomed to the simplicity of yes-and-no voting rather than the complex and more community-oriented consensus method of decision-making.

This process not only allows but encourages those who hold a minority view of the issue to fully explain why they hold this view. It allows for the majority to examine all aspects that could result in failure to reach the desired goal. The potential flaws or mistakes waiting to happen can be safely revealed and then be addressed, and the action plan can be modified to eliminate or reduce risk of failure.

What do the fist and numbers of fingers mean?

Asking participants to respond to an idea with either a fist or from one to five fingers illustrates the quality of "yes" indicators. A fist means "no," and any number of fingers is a "yes" with an indication of how good a "yes" it is. This moves a group away from quantity voting to quality voting, which gives the group more information.

- **A fist** means *I vote no. I object and will block consensus* (usually on moral grounds).
- **1 finger** means *I'll just barely go along, I don't like this but it's not quite a no*, or *I think there is a lot more work to do on this proposal.* In consensus this indicates standing aside, or not being in agreement but not blocking the consensus.
- **2 fingers** mean *I don't much like this but I'll go along.*
- **3 fingers** mean *I'm in the middle somewhere. Like some of it, but not all. I can live with it.*
- **4 fingers** mean *This is fine.*
- **5 fingers** mean *I like this a lot, and I think it's the best possible decision.*

Fist to Five Process:

1. You can use Fist to Five when an idea or proposal has been well discussed, there appears to be a majority, but concerns are still present. Instead of voting, call for Fist to Five. Your group can already have discussed the process previously, or you can explain it at the time needed.

2. Review what the fist and the various numbers of fingers actually mean, then ask the participants to raise their hands indicating what they think about the proposal at the current time. Ask them to hold their hands high so everyone can scan the room and see all.
3. Then ask each one who raised a fist or only one finger or two fingers to share their concerns or objections and offer possible solutions to overcome their objections, if they have some.
4. Allow some time for participants to ask clarifying questions or offer possible solutions for the stated objections.
5. This may result in some modifying of the proposal.
6. Ask the group again to raise their hands giving their indicators for the revised proposal or for the original one if no modifications were offered.
7. When you have all individuals with three fingers or more raised, you have reached a kind of consensus in that everyone *can live with it* and no further objections are being raised. This brings to the group the feeling that everyone can support the plan and there are no losers.
8. If you still have fists or one-finger indicators, you can repeat the process or move on to voting in a traditional manner with the majority prevailing.

Sometimes it is good to check for consensus early in a dialogue about a proposal because the group might be ready for consensus but are simply enjoying talking about it. An early check might, for example, find all four- and five-finger indicators except for two ones, meaning the proposal would be voted in, or, in the case of consensus, no one would block consensus and only two people have needs to be met. Only those people then speak and their objections can be addressed, which saves a lot of time.

If you have of a lot of ones, twos, and threes, it shows the group that the decision is probably a stopgap measure and will need to be watched closely or revisited soon. It is generally wise to attach a date for review to a decision that is low in quality. Some groups find it saves time in the end to not accept a vote that is affirmative but primarily ones and twos, as the proposal is generally troublesome and comes up again anyway.

If the vote is wildly split, with no real majority, the group knows it has more work to do and that the decision might not endure. They can expect more controversy and know a plan must be made to address the polarized views.

The benefits of managing conflict and gaining consensus:

- It can save time during seemingly unending discussions by gauging where everyone stands on an issue or decision.
- It actively pursues information from dissenters even if it is clear they are in the minority and could be outvoted.
- Revealing factors that could produce a failed project encourages more brainstorming on solving those issues in advance of a decision or a vote.
- Issues from dissenters can be addressed in action planning, and the dissenters can be converted into supporters.

> **A CHOICE TIP!**
>
> *Like attracts like. If we give up, so will others. If we cry, so will they. But if we decide this is a new beginning, others will take courage. We influence other people. Our attitudes send out ripples of feeling—like the scent of flowers that floats on air currents. What we think and say sets the stage for what is to happen. We can change our minds, our words, our attitudes, and we stop crying. We act like our prayers are already answered and take steps to show we believe it. When the early morning sun breaks through the far side of the woods, the dark places are lighted and much healing takes place. And so it is with us.*
>
> —Joyce Sequichie Hifler, *A Cherokee Feast of Days*

- The ultimate decision is strengthened by identifying potential weaknesses and addressing them.

Chapter 14

Some closing thoughts: think courage!

Inaction breeds doubt and fear. **Action** *breeds confidence and courage. If you want to conquer fear, do not sit home and think about it. Go out and get busy.*

—Dale Carnegie

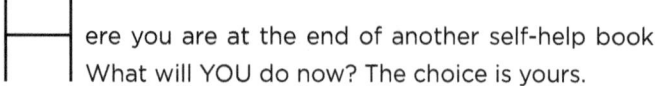

Here you are at the end of another self-help book. What will YOU do now? The choice is yours.

Whether you think conflict is good or bad, you create your own reality. When you begin to sense the messenger of conflict showing up in your life, remember that this is not *bad* news; it is *new information* showing up. Look for the truth in what's happening and then begin to look for the lessons that are present for all parties involved. This is a shift in consciousness.

When you don't understand why things are the way they are in your life, it is not always necessary to rush to find reasons. Sometimes trusting that everything is happening for a reason is much more powerful than knowing the reason. You can always communicate and cooperate with others to discover each others' expectations together.

The reasons for a problem might not matter—but knowing that you have a way to begin communicating about the change or problem does matter. You know now that you can begin by examining your own expectations, and then gently invite the others into a conversation to explore what they were expecting. What becomes more important is that the circumstances may now be present for a higher potential outcome than anyone involved was able to see before.

What happens if you don't manage change effectively or if you refuse to change?

Sometimes we hope the tensions that build before conflict will just go away if we ignore them. They rarely go away unless the person(s) and the relationship also go away.

We might think we can live with the tensions if they just stay the same and don't get worse. Experience demonstrates that if you don't choose to change or to manage change effectively, things will not just stay the same—they will likely get worse. The messenger of conflict will continue to knock at the door until it gets someone's attention and some subsequent action or reaction.

> *Being vulnerable doesn't have to be threatening. Just have the courage to be sincere, open and honest. This opens the door to deeper communication all around. It creates self-empowerment and the kind of connections with others we all want in life. Speaking from the heart frees us from the secrets that burden us. These secrets are what make us sick or fearful. Speaking truth helps you get clarity on your real heart directives.*
>
> —Sara Paddison, *The Hidden Power of the Heart*

Courage is an interesting word. It is defined as a quality of mind or spirit that enables one to face danger, fear, or uncertainties with self-possession, confidence, resolution, or bravery. The root word *corage* comes from French, *couer*, meaning heart. So we could say that it means the quality of heart that allows one to move forward without knowing the outcome. Courage is a form of maturity; it is the *coming of age of the heart*.

Heart is the operative word when *consciously choosing* to address, manage, or resolve conflict instead of ignoring it or hoping it will go away. It takes maturity of heart to confront one's own fears or insecurities, or the emotions of others. It takes maturity of heart to understand the power of choice—and then to choose wisely.

> *Courage is not the absence of fear but the awareness that something else is more important.*
>
> —Stephen Covey

Creating new habits also requires a certain level of courage. Most of us don't really think of habits when we are working our way through our daily lives. Our daily lives are filled with habits, and most of them are good, necessary, and lend themselves to a sense of order and well-being for ourselves and for others. Imagine what life would be like if we did not brush our teeth in the morning when we get up. It's a good habit!

It is when we feel alarmed or ashamed or receive feedback from others that something we are doing, thinking, or feeling is not in our best interests or is harmful to others that we are motivated to change. For many, the task of changing is one of a sense of the impossibility of climbing Mount Everest. We must gear up to *break* our bad habit.

Change is an exercise in freedom

Most of us are engaged in measuring our own rate of progress by human standards. Sometimes we believe that these habits cannot be changed. Where is the freedom in that? What hope is there for the world if people cannot search and cultivate the thoughts and feelings of their hearts to recognize personal opportunity and create their own environments?

Choosing to create movement is freedom! Being accountable for your choices is freedom! In a spiritual sense, mankind was given free will to choose and was encouraged to take dominion over our own world. When we fail to choose and just plug along allowing others to lower our standards of what life is to be, we are actually allowing our authority to lapse. Choosing not to commit, or harboring a sense of hopelessness about things ever changing, is a downward course. We cannot uphold the banner of our personal freedom if we do not make the most of our opportunity to choose to change and re-create ourselves, our families, our businesses, and our nations.

> *Courage is the commitment to begin without any guarantee of success.*
>
> —Goethe

Old patterns and habits form a groove. It is easier going to stay in a pathway—a groove—that is already well carved out. You encounter less resistance. Old habits can be like gravity—there is a natural pull to go the same old way and resist change.

When you choose to build a new habit, you have to break free of that gravitational pull. When you choose to stop doing something, like stop smoking or stop eating sugar, there is a void—a vacuum that is seeking to be filled immediately. What will you place in that vacuum? Identify and choose the thing or thought or feeling that you will choose to replace the old habit.

Keys to creating new habits:

- Recognize that creating something new requires will power—*free will* power. You are choosing by your own free will to change something, to create something new.

- Will power is like a muscle, and it can be trained to make it stronger.

- Will power appears to be stronger early in the day and wears down as the day winds down.

- When beginning something new, do it *every day at the same time for thirty days in a row*.

- Practice doing the new thing *early in the day* while you still have strong will power.

- Work on establishing *one new habit at a time*. If you add several at once, you are building in potential to fail or give up because it can feel overwhelming.

Habit patterns are in place in every area of life. They are not just nasty or annoying behaviors of which you or others disapprove. There are habits of emotional expression, of worded expression—everything that has to do with the organization of your life or what you do on a daily basis from morning until night. Sometimes we think that our habits or those of others are permanent—that they are a basic part of our temperament and therefore they cannot be changed. Imagine the freedom you can experience when you fully realize that, in fact, it was only a human habit and that you can just as easily shake that habit as you can take off an outworn garment.

You change your clothing daily, or for some, many times a day. You can surely change habits if you will just believe in transformation. The universe sends you stronger and stronger wake-up calls until you realize the necessity of personal transformation. Conflicts are wake-up calls. It's in your best interest to change proactively and recognize that the only person you are truly capable of changing is yourself.

> *Difficulties are meant to rouse, not discourage.*
> *The human spirit is to grow strong by conflict.*
>
> —William Ellery Channing

One of the most proactive ways to handle arguments and disagreements is to take a breath and ask, "What is this situation trying to teach me?" There is a lesson for all parties to learn.

> *Courage is the capacity to confront*
> *what can be imagined.*
>
> —Leo Rosten

Choose to believe, know that you can be the change agent in your own life, and move forward courageously to show others how to choose their own way.

> *Peace is not merely a distant goal that we seek, but a means by which we arrive at that goal. Martin Luther King Jr. said that, and he was right. And his wisdom holds true not only for peace in our world, but for peace within ourselves. All of our spiritual traditions teach the same thing. To achieve peace, be peace. Yet*

*how does one be what one is wishing to experience?
By a sheer act of Will. And... by causing others to
experience what you wish to experience.*

—Neale Donald Walsh

Appendix A

A simple action plan

If you fail to plan, you are planning to fail!
—Benjamin Franklin

Simply stated, an action plan is the stating of an objective followed by an outline of the tasks or actions needed to reach the objective. It also provides a timeline for completion of each action, who is responsible for that action, and the resources, both human and material, that are needed to complete the actions and the overall objective.

It can be as simple as a statement of who does what by when and what they need to do it. See the sample below.

OBJECTIVE:

Steps or Actions Needed	Person(s) Responsible	Date Needed
1.		
2.		
3.		
Resources (human and material) needed:		

Considerations for Action Plans with More Complex Objectives or More People Involved:

1. **Involvement:** Who needs to be involved in designing the action plan? This would include the affected people or their representatives or designees, and those responsible for decision-making and completion of the objective(s). Complete a list of all involved—names, contact information, and potential areas of contribution or responsibility.

2. **Critical information:** If the reason for action planning is due to an event or clear concern, identify and gather the information regarding the concern(s). Be specific.
3. **Needs assessment:** Review your objective(s) and decide if a needs assessment (surveys, inspections, complaints, investigations, etc.) will provide needed or helpful information.
4. **Identify changes needed:** Based on all the needs-assessment data you chose to collect, clearly articulate in writing what is needed to create positive or needed change.
5. **List the actions:** List the actions that are needed to meet these needs.
6. **Designate:** Designate the person(s) who will be responsible for completing these action steps.
7. **Timeline:** Create a timeline for each action to be completed.
8. **Resources needed:** Identify the human and material resources needed to complete the action plan.
9. **Evaluation:** Determine the date and place for a follow-up meeting for the group to review and evaluate progress toward implementing the action plan.
10. **Adjust:** Adjust and revise the action plan as needed.
11. **Knowledge identification:** Share what you as individuals and as a group have learned about yourself, your organization, your staff, your resources, and your ability to manage change from this action process. Document any necessary action items that can be a guide for you or others in the future.

Appendix B

When and how to use a summary memorandum

Why create a summary memo?

The purpose of creating a summary memo is to prevent conflict in the future. When people meet and speak with one another, each one tends to remember the things that are most important to them. And often we hear what we want to hear. The rest of the encounter can become hazy in our memories to the point of even denying that certain things were agreed to, discussed, or even mentioned.

The purpose of the summary memo is to capture briefly the most important things that were discussed and agreed to in a meeting or conversation between people. The agreements or decisions to take next steps are the most important.

Distribute the summary memo to all who attended, with directions to review and then respond by a certain time and date if there is anything missing or misstated. Include the statement that without a response, it will be considered by all that the information is correct. This summary memo can then be used later when memories might grow dim to help recall decisions made.

Key elements to include in a summary memo:

- Date the memo was written
- Names of those who attended and will receive the memo
- Author of the memo with signature or initial
- Date, time, and location of the meeting
- Purpose or objective for the meeting
- Main topic(s) of discussion; there is no need to include details.

- Any agreements or objectives regarding how things will be done or will proceed in the future, including details and next steps if necessary
- Any intentions for future meetings or follow-up
- The request that each person review the summary memo for accuracy and reply to all others if they feel something needs to be added or modified to be accurate. Include a date and time for receiving modifications.
- Use a delivery system that allows you to know that everyone received the memo; that is, email with return receipt that the email was read, registered postal mail, or ask that the memo be signed and returned to a specific address or location within the designated time frame.
- The originator of the summary memo should keep the original copy or see that it's filed with the group's records. Others might want to hold on to their copies for future reference.

About the author

Alberta Fredricksen is passionate about helping others use the presence of conflict to achieve fulfilling relationships and communicate more effectively. As a conflict and life coach and consultant, Alberta brings decades of experience to working with diverse individuals and groups. She has helped to empower people to effectively manage conflict in a wide variety of settings including families, employment settings, labor negotiations, a community mediation center, and non-profit organizations.

She has worked as a teacher, school administrator, mediator, human resource administrator, university instructor, consultant, coach, and minister, and is the author of books and articles on conflict resolution, personal development, and spirituality.

As the personnel director at a state prison, Alberta gained intensive experience in practical conflict-resolution skill-building, including negotiating with many unions; developing and implementing policies; investigating, facilitating, and resolving grievances; and supervising training programs.

Alberta strives to empower individuals to experience their highest potential while enhancing their connectedness with all of life.

For more information about Alberta Fredricksen and her work, visit her website at www.HeartPeaceNow.com

www.ingramcontent.com/pod-product-compliance
Lightning Source LLC
Chambersburg PA
CBHW062008070426
42451CB00008BA/272